labrador retriever

understanding and
caring for your dog

Written by
Ann Britton

labrador retriever

understanding and
caring for your dog

Written by
Ann Britton

Pet Book Publishing Company

Bishton Farm, Bishton Lane, Chepstow, NP16 7LG, United Kingdom.
881 Harmony Road, Unit A, Eatonton, GA31024 United States of America.

Printed and bound in China through Printworks International.

ISBN: 978-1-906305-58-1
ISBN: 1-906305-58-7

Acknowledgements

The publishers would like to thank the following for help with
photography: Ann Britton (Bowstones), Pat Davies (Holmajor), David
Coode (Warringah), Fiona Hilman (Penworlod), Erica Jayes (Sandylands);
David Tomlinson.

Page 11 © Guide Dogs for the Blind Association.
Pages 19, 65, 69, 73, 75, 91, 107, 115, 129, 141, 145, 161, 163, 179, and 183
© Sharon Rogers (www.woodmistlabradors.co.uk)
Page 49 © Zoe Rogers
Pages 99, and 192 © Sabine Stuewer (Tierfoto).

|Contents

Introducing the Labrador

The eager-to-please, fun-loving Labrador Retriever, known and loved by so many, is deservedly the most popular breed of dog in both the USA and the UK.

He is easy to care for, suffers few ills, and is a most loyal companion, who is faithful to the end of his days – normally, a life spanning 12 to 14 healthy years. I have a happy 16-year-old Lab sitting beside me as I write, proving that Labrador ownership is a long-term commitment.

When contemplating taking on a cuddly eight-week-old Labrador puppy, you should be aware that Labrador puppies quickly grow into lively medium-sized dogs, 21.5-22.5 inches (54-57 cm) in height and eventually weighing from 63-77 lb (28-35 kg). The Labrador is quick to learn and possesses the kindest of natures.

He is a multi-purpose dog, easily trained, and hence seen in the role of assistance dog, guide dog, or hearing dog. He has an outstanding sense of smell and performs search and rescue work as well being trained to sniff out drugs and explosives at ports and airports. In the countryside he is a steady, intelligent, shooting companion, and is an excellent swimmer and retriever.

However, for the majority of owners, the Labrador is their beloved, handsome pet dog and companion, trotting along on a country walk, playing with the family, digging sandcastles on the seashore and sharing the sandwiches.

On a cold winter's night he will happily cuddle up beside you on the sofa to watch TV, but be aware that he is likely to stretch out over the complete length of the sofa, leaving you with only the floor to sit on! In the summer, he is content to splash about in the paddling pool with the toddlers, or just laze in the shade on the lawn.

A Labrador loves human company – the more, the better. For loyalty, intelligence, ease of care and constant good humour, there is none to equal him. He is wonderful with children and especially gentle with those who are unwell.

He understands the human condition and is everyone's trustworthy friend to the end. Quite simply, the Labrador is a dog who will give years of pure devotion.

Retrieving is a passion, and this is not confined to toys – books, papers, the TV remote, abandoned shoes, and the contents of the laundry bin – all may, at some time, be found neatly collected together in your Labrador's bed, hopefully not chewed.

The Labrador is one of life's great enthusiasts. He will literally bowl you over when he greets you, unless he is properly trained, and his ever-wagging tail will sweep the contents of a coffee table on to the floor in seconds. Water is an irresistible attraction. The Labrador has an uncanny gift for detecting it from miles away and plunging in before you can stop him, so travelling home with a wet dog in the car is part of a Labrador' owner's way of life.

Right: The versatile Labrador is highly valued as an assistance dog, helping people with disabilities.

One thing, which has to be watched throughout a Labrador's life, is his waistline. A Labrador adores food and has the ability to melt your heart with one imploring look. He will easily convince you that he is suffering extreme hunger and needs just one more treat. Unfortunately, where food is concerned, Labradors are morally challenged; their self-service instinct is extremely well developed. But otherwise, he is canine perfection and rightly the choice of millions all over the world.

If you want an outstanding family companion, look no further...

Tracing back in time

It is intriguing to look back over the centuries to find out how the breed evolved, for the exact origins are far from clear.

Some 200 years ago the Labrador's ancestors came to Britain from Newfoundland Island, which is situated just south of Labrador on the rugged east coast of Canada.

Evidence suggests that in 1000 AD, Viking explorers sailed to mainland Labrador and to Newfoundland Island. Later centuries saw the island occupied by Beothuck Indians. However, there was no record of any resident dogs in the area during these times.

In the 15th and 16th centuries, in Europe, more than 2,000 miles away on the other side of the Atlantic Ocean, dogs similar to present-day Labradors were depicted in splendid Spanish, Italian and Portuguese oil paintings, often standing next to, or lying at the

foot of, the subject of the painting – a person of noble birth.

The 16th century was a time when European explorers travelled the world by sea, and traders regularly sailed back and forth between continents. Fishing fleets crossed the Atlantic Ocean to trawl the rich cod banks off Newfoundland. On board ship, included as part of the working crew, were their working dogs. Did these dogs perhaps resemble the dogs from the noble European paintings and were they the forerunners of the Labrador?

The sea around Newfoundland Island is chilled by the Labrador current which flows south from the Arctic Circle. Fishing in the cod-filled waters of the Grand Banks proved so plentiful that, over the years, fishermen from England, and later Portugal and Spain, settled for good at St Johns in the south-east of Newfoundland. Of course, the working dogs, which travelled with them across the ocean, stayed too.

Two types emerge

Over time, the settlers' dogs bred with local dogs. Probably these had also arrived in Newfoundland via ships from various parts of the world. Two distinct types of dog evolved in the area, and 19th century writers talk of the Newfoundland Dog (similar to today's Newfoundland) and the Lesser Newfoundland Dog, also known as the St John's Dog, ancestor of the Labrador.

In the early 1800s, a renowned wildfowler, Colonel Peter Hawker, an Englishman, who was one of the foremost shooting sportsmen of the time, owned a trading schooner. It sailed back and forth across the Atlantic Ocean between Poole, on the south coast of England, and Newfoundland Island. He observed and wrote about the two types of dog which inhabited Newfoundland.

In 1814 in his book, *Instructions to Young Sportsmen,* he described the Newfoundland Dog as: "a very large dog, strong of limb, with rough hair and carrying his tail high." These dogs were the ancestors of today's Newfoundlands. The other type of dog, the Lesser Newfoundland Dog or St John's Dog, the forebear of our Labradors, Colonel Hawker described as:

"...by far the best for any kind of shooting dog. He is generally black and no bigger than a Pointer, very fine in legs, with short, smooth hair and

The larger heavier dogs evolved into the Newfoundland we know today.

does not carry his tail so much curled as the other, (Newfoundland); he is extremely quick, running, swimming... his sense of smell is hardly to be credited. In finding wounded game there is not a living equal in the canine race. He is chiefly used on the native coast by fishermen...."

The perfect working retriever

The St John's Dog's short, thick, waterproof coat, which repelled ice, (unlike that of his larger, hairier cousin, the Newfoundland), his swimming ability, coupled with his strength, trainability and utter enthusiasm for life meant that the dogs were excellent workers and an important part of the fishing trade. Being tough, hardy and medium-sized, they happily toiled alongside the fishermen, in the chilly climate. Swimming in the freezing cold waters, they retrieved cod that had escaped from the fishing hooks or nets. They rescued crew members who had fallen overboard and they fetched objects that had slipped into the water. They hauled in the fishing nets, and, at the end of the day, towed the fishing boats ashore, up the shelved beaches, to be moored safely for the night.

There are tales of foggy days when, to avoid collision, a St John's Dog sitting beside a fisherman in his boat, would bark to alert others of their location; stories tell of dogs swimming considerable distances from one

The Labrador was an invaluable helpmate to Newfoundland's fishermen.

boat to another, carrying messages. On land they were even used to haul wood on sledges from inaccessible places. The wood was then stacked and later used to smoke fish. It appears the St John's Dog could turn his paw to any job required! Newfoundland was also home to a plentiful source of game birds. The settlers found the St John's Dogs were ideal hunting companions, easily retrieving the shot game.

Such was the dogs' energy, their compliant nature and enthusiasm for life that having finished one job, they were always ready and waiting for the next. By the end of the day, still in excellent humour, they were quite content to settle down to relax and amuse the family's children.

I know many of you who own Labradors today will recognise so many of these endearing characteristics, including their love of water, of retrieving and delight in human companionship – all inherited directly from the St John's Dogs.

The Labrador's love of
water dates back to
his days as
fisherman's mate.

Developing the breed

In the early 1800s, trading ships returning from Newfoundland to England carried St John's Dogs back to the UK. Such was their reputation as sportsmen's dogs, being excellent swimmers and retrievers, they were quickly acquired by the sporting aristocracy.

The 2nd Earl of Malmesbury of Heron Court, near Poole, acquired St John's Dogs from trading ships returning to Poole harbour, and he established his kennel, based solely on pure St. John's Dogs, in the early years of the 19th century. His son, the 3rd Earl of Malmesbury, born in 1807, also imported and bred purely from the St John's Dogs, never crossing with other breeds. He called the dogs he bred Labradors.

Just as had been seen in Newfoundland, the 3rd Earl recognized his Labradors' great potential

as highly accomplished retrievers. They had a particular type and character of their own, which he wanted to preserve: working over the wet and marshy duck-shooting grounds of his estates, his dogs proved their worth. Colonel Peter Hawker, who had observed the St John's Dogs in Newfoundland so many years before, continued to import them for the Earl of Malmesbury's breeding programme until 1875.

The Scottish link

While, in the south of England, the 2nd and 3rd Earls of Malmesbury were breeding from their St Johns' Dogs, in the Scottish Borders, keen sportsmen – the 5th Duke of Buccleuch (born 1806) and his brother, Lord John Scott (born 1809), plus the Earls of Home and their families – had also been importing and breeding pure St John's Dogs.

These Scottish, Victorian aristocrats certainly enjoyed the companionship of their Labradors, just as we do now. In 1839, many years before the Quarantine Act was introduced to prevent the spread of rabies from mainland Europe to Britain, the 5th Duke of Buccleuch sailed on his yacht to Naples with his black Labrador, Moss, accompanied by the 10th Earl of Home and his black Labrador, Drake.

One of the early photographs of a Labrador is of the 11th Earl of Home's black bitch, Nell, taken in 1867

when she was 12 years of age. It shows a typical Labrador of the time, used for shooting in England and Scotland. She was black-coated with a pure white muzzle and four pure white feet, and, apart from the white, looking not so very different to our present-day black Labradors.

Forging a Link

In the early 1880s, the 6th Duke of Buccleuch and the 12th Earl of Home were visiting Bournemouth during the winter and joined a shooting party on the Malmesbury estate. Observing the Earl of Malmesbury's dogs, they were amazed at the way they worked, especially in water. These dogs, although based on the same pure St John's Dogs as their own Scottish dogs, were in a totally different category. The Earl of Malmesbury made a gift of three of his homebred Labradors to the Scottish Buccleuch kennels: Ned (born in 1882) and Avon (born 1885) and Nell (birthdate unknown), and this established a strong link between the two kennels.

With great enthusiasm, a joint breeding programme was established between the Scottish Buccleuch and Home kennels, and the English kennel of the Earl of Malmesbury. When the bloodlines were combined, an excellent Labrador Retriever strain developed with a consistency in type from one generation to the next.

The three Labrador colors: Black, Yellow, and Chocolate.

From 1882, all breeding records were noted down and these formed the first Labrador studbook.

In 1888, Lord George Scott, younger son of the 6th Duke of Buccleuch, took over the management of the Buccleuch Labradors in Scotland. At that time there were more than 60 gamekeepers on 450,000 acres of the various Buccleuch estates. Within a few years, every Buccleuch gamekeeper was provided with one or more purebred Labradors. Such was Lord George Scott's enthusiasm for the breed that he planned all the matings and oversaw the rearing of all the puppies, so that the correct type of Labrador, to which he and his family and friends had devoted so much time and effort, was maintained.

The establishment of good bloodlines in Britain proved essential, as, by 1885, imports of dogs to England from Newfoundland had subsided, and by the middle of the 20th century, in its homeland of Newfoundland, the St John's Dogs became extinct. However, the Labrador's future in Britain was assured thanks to the dedication of the Earls of Malmesbury, Home and the Dukes of Buccleugh and their families and friends. The Labrador's reputation as a retriever was already beginning to outstrip that of the highly regarded, black Wavy Coated Retriever.

Coat colors

The three colors – black, yellow and chocolate (originally called liver) – have existed from the early days of the 19th century dog from Newfoundland Island. It is probable that the imported St John's Dogs carried the gene for all three colors. However, the Victorian breeders in England and Scotland generally selected for the black coat color, culling the majority of pups of other colors.

In 1892 the birth of the first liver puppies was recorded. Although colors other than black had appeared in litters prior to this date, liver and yellow puppies were not in demand. The first two recorded liver puppies were sired by Buccleugh Avon, who was one of the three dogs initially given by the Earl of Malmesbury to the Duke of Buccleugh. Thus, Buccleugh Avon is probably behind many of today's popular chocolate Labradors.

In 1899 the first recorded yellow, Ben of Hyde, was born in a litter of black puppies from two black parents at Major Radcliff's kennel. This dog was the foundation of the early yellow Labrador kennels.

Naming the breed

No one really knows for certain how the Labrador Retriever got its name. Obviously, the Retriever part is clear, but how the name Labrador came about may be quite accidental.

Is it possible it was it a simple geographical mistake? Perhaps the English aristocrats who imported the first St John's Dogs were uncertain of the precise geographical location of the island of Newfoundland. Mistakenly they may have thought it was part of neighboring Labrador.

Another suggestion is that early pictures of the Portuguese workers' dog, Cane di Castro Laboreiro, show a very marked similarity to the Labrador.

Did Portuguese sailors arrive in Newfoundland bringing with them their Laboreiro? Did they cross those dogs with those of the English settlers? Did the title Labrador come from the name Laboreiro ('labourer')? We will never know.

Breed recognition

The Kennel Club in the UK was established in 1873. Retrievers in the Kennel Club Stud Books were listed together under one general Retriever section, with no separation between breeds. Therefore, it was possible to register half the pups from a litter as Golden Retrievers and the other half as Labradors! In 1903 the KC finally listed the Labrador Retriever as a separate breed, and in 1916 the Labrador Retriever Club was formed. The American Kennel Club registered their first Labrador in 1917 – a female called Brocklehirst Nell from Munden bloodlines. Official recognition came in the 1920s and the American Labrador Retriever Club was founded in 1931.

The breed was imported to the UK in a small way before World War One, but numbers increased dramatically in the 1920s when word of the Labrador's working abilities spread. Rich landowners on the east side of the USA not only imported the breed, they set up shooting estates on British lines and brought in gamekeepers from the UK – and particularly from Scotland – to run them. These gamekeepers brought their own Labradors with them – and so the gene pool was further enriched.

These early imports provided the breed's foundation in North America, and from the World War II onwards, it went from strength to strength in both countries.

The Labrador is still valued as one of the finest dogs on the shooting field.

What should a Labrador look like?

All pedigree dog breeds have their a 'Breed Standard' – a written blueprint describing the 'perfect' specimen. Breeders strive to produce dogs that conform to the Standard, and in the show ring the judge will be looking for the dog that best fits the Standard.

Dogs that win in the ring will be used for breeding. It is vital that only the very best are used to produce future generations, preserving the breed as it is meant to be.

Breed characteristics

The Standard ensures the Labrador is built to perform his task as a gundog for long hours, picking up and

carrying heavy game without strain. His intelligent, kind temperament and ease of training make him popular with sportsmen and pet owners alike.

The outline should be clean in profile; broad with plenty of heart room when viewed from the front; strong and muscular when viewed from the rear. He should be a strongly built, well-balanced, short coupled, active dog; a sturdy animal with substance and energy.

Head and skull

The skull is broad with a definite stop, which is the point where the forehead meets the muzzle. The length of the skull from the occiput (the slightly raised point at the centre-back of the skull) to the stop is similar to the length of the muzzle, which should be broad and level, not snipey, when viewed from the top and the side. The nostrils should be wide.

The eyes are almond-shaped and set square in the skull, neither slanted upwards nor downwards. They are brown – the color of burnt sugar – and their melting expression reflects kindness and intelligence.

The ears, which are soft as velvet, are set well back. Ideally, if held across the eye on the same side, the ear should just reach the inner corner of that eye.

Points of anatomy

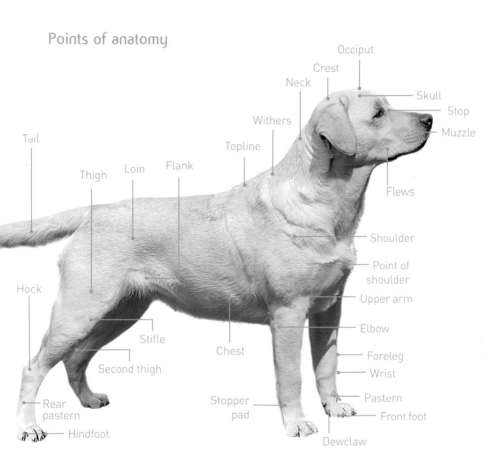

Occiput

Crest

Neck

Skull

Stop

Withers

Muzzle

Topline

Flews

Tail

Thigh

Loin

Flank

Shoulder

Point of shoulder

Upper arm

Hock

Elbow

Stifle

Foreleg

Second thigh

Chest

Wrist

Rear pastern

Pastern

Stopper pad

Front foot

Hindfoot

Dewclaw

A scissor bite is required, with the top teeth closely overlapping the bottom teeth. The Labrador should have 42 strong, white teeth.

Neck

The neckline should flow into a level topline with no sharp angles.   An imaginary marble, placed at the top of the neck, should roll slowly down the neck across the shoulder, level topline and quarters to the tail, without falling off.

The neck is of medium length, longer on top than underneath. The throat is clean, with no excess hanging skin, known as throatiness.

There should be no rucks or unsightly rolls across his shoulder, pointing to either imperfect front construction, or excess weight and lack of coat.

Front construction

If this is correct, the Labrador can perform his task as a gundog with ease; if it is wrong, he will constantly jar himself, as he will have no springing to cushion his movement. Look for the front construction triangle, which holds the secret. If the front is made right, the rest will normally follow:

The first side of the triangle is a vertical line dropped from the shoulder at the withers (where the top

The Labrador has a broad skull, with ears set well back and eyes the color of burnt sugar.

of the neckline meets the back). This vertical line should pass through the back of the elbow. If the line falls well behind the elbow, even though the dog's shoulder blade may be of the correct length and angle, the upper arm will be too short and upright.

The second side of the triangle is the shoulder blade. Of good length, it leaves the withers, slopes down to the point of shoulder at the front of the chest, where it makes a 90-degree angle with the upper arm. If it is too short, the dog will have difficulty picking up heavy objects.

The third side of the triangle is the upper arm, between the elbow joint and the point of shoulder. This bone is often too short and instead of being angled forward is almost upright, which gives the dog no spring when moving and instead results in jarring. If the upper arm construction is incorrect, the Labrador will move with short, rapid 'dolly steps' instead of easy, energy-saving strides. The upper arm should be at an angle of 145 degrees to the vertical foreleg at the elbow; the angle of a policeman's arm held high, having instructed you to halt!

Front legs

From the side, leg length should reflect a proportion of 50/50 withers to elbow, elbow to ground Well-boned forelegs are strong and straight. Excessive bone is incorrect, as is weak spindly bone.

If front construction is correct, the overall conformation is likely to be correct.

Pasterns (located below the wrist) are strong with slight flexibility. The bone above and below the pastern should be the same, not tapering. The feet should face forward, not turning out or in, with neat, well-arched toes and well-developed pads.

Body

The ribcage is wide, well sprung and barrel shaped, of good length, especially in breeding bitches. Slab sides, where the ribcage is flat, are incorrect, as are short ribcages with little length from front to back. The topline should be level with the no dipping behind the shoulder.

The chest is deep and wide, the brisket between the forelegs coming down at least to the level of the elbow.

The Labrador is short-coupled, to ensure the loin, the area between the back of the ribs and the quarters, is strong. He should be neither too fat nor too thin, but well covered with some sign of a waist.

Hindquarters

Viewed from above, the hindquarters are wider than the front assembly. They are broad and strong, not falling away at the croup; the tail comes straight off the back. From the rear the quarters should be wide, strong and well-muscled.

In profile, the well-developed second thighs should resemble the shape of a generous ham. There should be a good bend of stifle but not an over-angulated stifle, which sets the leg too far back, causing weakness.

The hocks should be well let down and perpendicular to the ground, neither sloping in under the body (sickle hocks) not set excessively far back.

Tail

This is described as an otter tail and is used for balance when swimming. It is well covered with coat, without feathering, It reaches to the hock and is wide at the root gradually tapering to a point.

Movement

Correct construction produces straight, true, driving movement with unexaggerated, ground covering, easy-flowing strides.

The Labrador is short coupled with a deep, wide chest.

The forelegs should come straight forwards, neither pinning in, towards each other, caused by being 'out at elbow', nor with outwardly flapping feet from being 'tied at elbow'. Hind movement should be square, converging slightly with pace. Faulty construction includes: too wide behind; cow-hocks, which produce a sideways thrust rather than forwards impulsion; rubbing hocks, which are so close together they almost brush; crossing hind feet.

Coat and colors

The waterproof coat of the Labrador is a short-length, double coat; a harsh topcoat overlying a dense soft, woolly undercoat; never open textured. The recognized colors are whole-colored black, yellow and chocolate.

Breed essentials

The Labrador must look like a Labrador and no other breed of dog. The Labrador 'must haves' are:

- A kind temperament.

- A beautifully chiselled shape to his broad head and muzzle, featuring a soft, gentle expression with warm, brown, burnt-sugar colored eyes.

- A double coat, harsh on top with woolly undercoat.

- An otter tail.

The essential Labrador combining the conformation and character that makes the breed unique.

What do you want from your Labrador?

No matter what plans you have for your Labrador, he should always be regarded, first and foremost, as a lifetime companion – and any other ambitions you have should be of secondary importance.

However, it makes sense to find the dog that is most likely to fit your lifestyle, and so you need to decide, in your own mind, what you are looking for.

Show dog

If you plan to show your Labrador, you need to find a puppy that has show potential. This means the pup has the correct structure and movement at an early stage of his development, which gives him the best chance of maturing into an adult of show quality.

There are absolutely no guarantees that a puppy will fulfil his early potential, but if you research the bloodlines of top show kennels, tracing back through the generations, you will form an idea of the type of pup that is likely to be produced.

Keep studying the Breed Standard (see pages 34-45) so you understand what is considered correct and what are faults in a show dog.

Working dog

The Labrador was bred to be the supreme retriever, fetching fallen game from land and from water. He needed to work closely with his owner, and so a biddable nature was essential.

These basic requirements are still prized by the shooting fraternity, and Labradors remain a popular choice as working gundogs.

In both the USA and the UK, there has been a divergence between Labradors bred for conformation classes in the show ring and thus fitting the Breed Standard, and those bred purely for their working ability in the shooting field, who come in all shapes and sizes.

In general, a Labrador bred from working lines is lighter in build, and often has a narrower head. Colors may also differ; there are few chocolate Labradors from working lines, and yellow Labradors are often darker, coming in a shade known as fox red, which is allowed in the show ring but rarely seen.

If you want to compete in one of the canine sports, such as Obedience, Tracking, Flyball or Agility, you should consider getting a Labrador from working lines as they more likely to have the drive that is needed.

Companion

The vast majority of Labradors that are produced go to pet homes and provide wonderful companionship. In my opinion, the laid-back show-bred Labrador makes the perfect pet. Some working-bred Labradors settle down well as pets, too, but others can be very busy animals who would rather live outside in a kennel, performing the working task their ancestors were initially bred for, rather than sitting quietly, in comfort, by the fireside.

If you are choosing a Labrador as a pet, a minor fault – such as incorrect tail carriage – would rule him out as a show dog, but would be of no significance in a companion dog. For this reason it is important to make sure the breeder knows exactly what you are looking for.

Temperament should always be an important consideration but it is the top priority when choosing a companion dog.

What does your Labrador want from you?

A Labrador's demands are few; his short coat and easy-going nature means that he is a relatively low-maintenance breed. However, like all living animals he has his own special needs, of which you should be fully aware before taking the plunge into Labrador ownership.

A lifetime's commitment

A Labrador lives between 12 and 14 years. Do you have room in your life and your home for this lifelong commitment? When your Labrador is young, he will want activity; in his later years, he will want a gentle stroll and a warm, comfy bed to snooze in.

Throughout your Labrador's life, you are responsible for providing his food, paying for vet bills and other expenses, such as boarding kennels when you go on holiday. Make sure you can afford to do this.

Companionship

Labradors thrive on human company. It is not kind to take a dog on and then leave him at home on his own all day long with no company. In fact, if everyone is out at work from 9am till 5pm, it would be better to forget the dog-owning idea for a while and wait until circumstances change before proceeding. A bored, lonely Labrador will find mischief to keep himself occupied; he may become destructive or he may drive the neighbors mad by barking and whining.

No dog should be left for more than four hours at a time. If you need to leave your Lab for longer periods you will have to make other arrangements, such as employing a dog-sitter or a dog-walker. Some working owners opt for doggy day care – but you will need to check out the facilities and the people running them – to ensure your Labrador will receive the care he needs.

A place of safety

Labradors can clear medium-height fences quite easily, if they are so inclined. The garden fence should be at least 5-6 ft high (1.5-1.8 metres); ideally, a close-boarded wooden fence on concrete, or stout wooden posts. Do not use chain-link fencing, as it is easy for the dog to unravel. You will also need to check that gates are protected at the sides and at the bottom. Remember, it only takes a split second for a puppy to get out and be run over by a passing car.

Exercise and mental stimulation

The Labrador is built on athletic lines, bred to work for long days in the field. In order to maintain the correct weight, he must have regular, varied exercise.

A Labrador needs no formal exercise until he is six months old, but it is worth taking him to a local park to exercise on a lead. Never let him run free or with other dogs until he is much older as this could damage his growing joints.

Below: Can you give your Labrador the time and attention he deserves?

Once your Labrador is fully grown, you must give him at least two walks a day – regardless of the weather. This should be a combination of lead walking and free running exercise, as long as you are in a safe place. Remember that exercise provides mental stimulation as well as physical exertion, so try to introduce variety – going to different places so that your Lab can enjoy investigating new sights and smells.

See Exercise Guidelines, page 122.

Training and socialization

A Labrador does not arrive as a model canine citizen – it takes hard work, time and patience to rear a puppy so that he becomes a well-behaved adult.

To begin with your puppy will need to be socialized so that he gets used to the sights and sounds of everyday life. If you do not have children in the family, you must make sure he has the opportunity to meet them, as well as getting used to visitors coming to your home.

Once your puppy has completed his vaccinations (see page 156), you can take him to the local park so he can socialize with other dogs and also meet their owners; he should also go to the shops so he can get used to crowds of people and the sound of traffic.

Socialization is vitally important in the first 12 months but it should be regarded as an on-going process that continues throughout your Labrador's life.

You will also need to spend time training your Labrador. This may seem more like something you want from your Labrador rather than the other way round. However, an adult dog that understands his boundaries and knows what is expected of him will be a more settled individual. He will enjoy spending quality time with you, and will relish the opportunity to use his brain.

Color
choices

Labradors come in three colors: yellow, black and chocolate. No other colors are recognised. People generally think that a litter would be all of the same whole-colored puppies (i.e. all black pups or all yellow or all chocolate), but if both parents carry the genes for the three colors, then in all probability there will be representatives of each color within the litter.

The only times when all the puppies in a litter are the same color are either when both parents are yellow themselves (in which case all the puppies are yellow), or if one of the parents is dominant black, in which case all the puppies are black. Other than these exceptions, there is often the chance of black, chocolate and yellow puppies appearing in a litter.

Black

This is the traditional Labrador color, so popular and successful in the show ring, the shooting field, and as wonderful, faithful pets. The black coat is double – harsh on top with a woolly undercoat, which is often mouse-grey in color. A single, shiny black coat with no woolly undercoat is incorrect. The coat is to keep the dog warm and dry.

Black Labradors are quick to learn and I find them most intelligent. They moult twice a year, in spring and in the autumn. In addition to this, bitches usually moult 19 weeks after their season, whether mated or not. Once moulting starts, it will be three months before the coat is fully returned.

Chocolate

Although the first chocolate Labradors were registered in 1892, the color was not popular. It was not until the 1980s that the color came to the fore, and since then chocolate Labradors have been in great demand as pets, bizarrely often commanding a higher price for their initial rarity, than excellent, top-quality animals of the other coat colors.

Unfortunately, because of this price excess, puppy farms have concentrated on breeding chocolate Labradors and so if you are looking for this color, you must be very careful to check out the breeder. Luckily, there are now many excellent show kennels which produce top-class chocolate Labradors. When looking at an adult, chocolate Labrador, ideally they should have an even-colored dark brown double coat, dark brown pigment, and brown eyes.

Chocolates make good pets but have been less successful in the show ring as not everyone appreciates the color. However among those exhibited, some have achieved considerable success.

Chocolate Labradors moult the same as black Labradors – twice yearly – and bitches normally 19 weeks after their season, whether or not they have had puppies. When exposed to strong summer sunshine, the dark chocolate color is known to fade towards ginger or yellow, somewhat patchily on the head and body.

Yellow

These are the glamour boys and girls of the breed, with the color ranging from pale cream to dark fox red.

The yellows make the most adorable pets, are top winners in the show ring, and work well in the shooting field. They have the best of temperaments (kindness itself), they are placid and extremely loving. Nothing fazes them. I often think their main thought is, "How's my hair looking today?" as they lazily smile and pat an ear with a paw. They are surely on this earth just to have a lovely, comfy life!

Yellows have the same double coat as the blacks and chocolates. They usually moult twice yearly and bitches 19 weeks after their season.

Extra considerations

Before you start your search for a Labrador, there are a few more important decisions to make, such as sex, age and how many.

Male or female

The choice of a male or female Labrador is very much a matter of personal preference, but there are a few points to consider.

Males

The Labrador male makes a lifelong, faithful, lovable friend. He is strong, jovial, hale and hearty, and loves his human family every single moment of his happy life. You will be his idol from the minute you meet.

At about 12 months of age he can become a bit of a silly teenager with eyes only for the girls, but this period is quickly over and he soon settles down to a

life of pure devotion to his human family.

Once he is fully mature, you may decide to have your male neutered (castrated); this does have some health benefits but should not be seen as a solution to behavioral problems. The best plan is to discuss the pros and cons of neutering with your vet.

Females

Bitches are most endearing and they, too, make delightful pets. Neater and possibly more gentle and fastidious, they are smaller than the dogs, usually by about 50 mm at the shoulder. They therefore weigh less.

Unspayed females come 'in season' or 'on heat' (ready for mating) once every six to eight months for a three-week period.

Once your Labrador has finished maturing (at around 18 months) and had at least one season (which may make her as old as 24 months), you may consider spaying her. This has considerable health benefits, but it can bring about the growth of a heavy woolly coat, and there is the possibility of weight gain, which can be controlled by monitoring food intake. Some bitches may experience urinary incontinence as they get older, though often this can be treated by your vet.

An older dog

In most cases, people opt for buying a puppy, but it may suit your lifestyle to take on an older dog or a rescued dog that needs rehoming.

Sometimes there is an opportunity to buy a slightly older, 'pick of the litter' puppy – a special pup, run on to show by the breeder. Perhaps the pup has not made the grade for the show ring for some minor cosmetic reason; maybe he carries his tail too high, or too low; perhaps his ears are on the large side. Some dogs do not take to the show ring; they are bored with it, and give the clear impression they would rather be enjoying the outdoors, swimming in the pond or walking in the hills. This is a wonderful chance to buy a really top-class puppy, one who would never have been available to purchase as a pet, from a show kennel at eight weeks of age.

You may decide you would like to rehome a dog from a rescue centre and give him a second chance in life. Some arrive at the rescue centre's door through sad circumstances, such as the divorce or death of their owners. Other dogs come from owners who, for one reason or another, should probably never have taken on a Labrador in the first place. At some point they decide they do not want their Labrador any more, often for the flimsiest of reasons. "Oh, we're going on holiday", or "It's Christmas, we're having a new settee!"

If you apply for a rescued dog, be prepared for your home and lifestyle to be thoroughly vetted by the rescue organizers. This is not an insult but has to be done to ensure that the home is permanent, suitable and that, once rehomed, these formerly unfortunate dogs will live a long, happy, fulfilled life with you and never suffer upheaval again.

More than one?

Labradors love the company of other dogs. Two Labradors in a household are ideal. They keep each other company and are happy and contented when you are out. If you do aim to have two, just make sure that your first Labrador is at least two years of age before you take on the second.

Two together?

I would never advise acquiring two pups from the same litter or two pups of exactly the same age. The reason for this is that as they grow and get heavier, enthusiastic, under two-year-old Labradors can play very roughly with each other, albeit always in fun. They can charge around at great speed together, like motorcyclists in a race. These carefree games can get out of hand. The youngsters do not know their own strength and can easily crash into each other or fall awkwardly. A glancing collision at full gallop could well damage their growing joints, possibly causing lameness in later life.

My advice is to concentrate on rearing the first pup safely and correctly, and then, when he is about two to three years of age and much more steady and sensible, think about getting him a puppy companion.

At the other end of the age-scale, an old Labrador is rejuvenated by the arrival of a young puppy in his home. He takes on a completely new role in life as wise puppy-minder. He teaches the youngster the rules of the house and, in so doing, he himself becomes less sedate for finding a new reason for living.

Resist the temptation of taking on two puppies from the same litter.

Sourcing a puppy

Your Labrador will be with you and your family for a very long time, and so you should be prepared to put time and effort into finding a puppy. Buyers travel hundreds of miles to find their special puppy; your chosen breeder may not necessarily be the nearest Labrador kennel to your home address.

So where do you go to find a typical, healthy Labrador? The best place to start searching is with your national Kennel Club. Both the Kennel Club in the UK and the American Kennel Club have excellent websites that provide details of breed clubs, lists of assured Labrador breeders, and also breeders that have puppies available. There are various schemes that have been designed to encourage reputable breeding and rearing practices. Genuine breeders will adhere to a strict code of ethics and carry out health checks on their breeding stock.

Alternatively, you can contact the Labrador breed clubs direct, which will have details of breeders with puppies available – all from health-checked parents.

If you want to work your Labrador, you will need to go to a specialist breeder who has a reputation for producing sound, healthy dogs that are reliable workers, or have made their mark in Field Trials (see page 154).

Buyer beware

Be wary about answering advertisements in local papers, or searching the Internet for puppies, as you may well fall into the hands of unscrupulous breeders who are producing puppies purely for gain. It is unlikely that breeding stock will have been health tested, and the puppies are unlikely to have received the care and attention they need to get off to a good start in life.

Over a lifetime, it costs less to feed and house a well-bred, healthy Labrador from health-checked parents for up to 14 years, than to care for a poor, sickly example, who hardly resembles the breed, has no papers, no health checks, and requires frequent and expensive veterinary attention throughout his life.

Health screening

We are fortunate that the Labrador is a healthy breed and has relatively few breed-specific health issues. However, it is essential that the parents of your puppy are health checked. This includes scoring hips and possibly elbows, eye tests and DNA tests. When you go to see the breeder, ask to see the health certificates and check that the dates are current.

For detailed information see Inherited and Breed disposed disorders, page 182.

Be on your guard for unscrupulous breeders who care more about money than the welfare of the puppies they produce.

Puppy
watching

Arrange to see the breeder when the puppies are about five weeks of age and their individual personalities have started to emerge.

What to look for

When you visit the breeder, you will be able to meet one or both of the health-checked parents. In most cases, the father (sire) will not be on the premises, as the breeder will probably have travelled some distance to find the best stud dog for his bitch.

The mother of the pups will be on the premises. Hormonal changes after the birth may mean she is not in the best of coat when you visit, but she should appear bright-eyed, fit and well, and certainly not look dirty, drained, exhausted or thin. In all likelihood, she will greet you with her tail wagging happily and be proud to show you her lovely babies. It is very important to check that she has a good, sound temperament, as this will have a significant influence on the puppies she has produced.

You may also get to see close relatives of the mother and her puppies, and this will help you to get a better idea of the type of dogs that come from these bloodlines.

When you arrive, the puppies may be playing or be fast asleep. They should be living in clean conditions and, once awake, they should appear bright eyed, happy, and look you straight in the eye, which is a sign of good character. They should be alert and inquisitive, not timid. They will have been wormed already so should look healthy and well rounded.

Making the choice

The breeder will have spent hours watching the pups and will know each one individually. For this reason, it is best to be guided by them as they are most likely to know the pup that is most suitable for your lifestyle.

If you are looking for a puppy to show, the breeder will help you to assess conformation and go over the points of the Breed Standard. If possible, ask someone who has experience in the breed to come with you . As well as having the correct structure, a show puppy should have a certain style in the way he holds himself when moving. He needs an extrovert character, a perfect temperament, and he really must have that X Factor!

If you go to a breeder that specializes in producing working puppies, again, you should be guided by their expert knowledge. Be clear about your ambitions, and this will help the breeder to pinpoint the right puppy.

As a general rule, you are looking for a lively pup who is keen to interact with you, and mad about retrieving!

The breeder will also ask you lots of questions about your home and lifestyle. Do not be offended – a responsible breeder will have put a great deal of care and effort into rearing the puppies and will want them to go to reliable, permanent homes where there is no risk that the puppy will become surplus to requirements and returned for rehoming later.

Puppy pack

To get you and your puppy off to the best start, the breeder will put together a puppy pack, which will be ready when you collect your puppy. This will include:

- A written pedigree – this will usually go back at least five generations.

- Kennel Club registration papers.

- Copies of the health certificates of both parents.

- Temporary insurance certificate.

- A contract of sale which you will need to sign.

- Details of worming/flea treatments to date.

- A diet sheet detailing what the pup has been fed and giving guidelines for the next 12 months.

- A sample of feed to last for the first few days.

- Contact details for after sales help and advice.

A puppy from working lines should be playful and keen to interact with you.

Getting ready

Once your Labrador puppy or adult is booked, you have about three weeks to sort out all the practical things needing attention around your house and garden before he arrives.

In the garden

Labradors are intelligent, inquisitive dogs, who usually think one step ahead of you. Your garden must be well fenced and totally secure. Fence off all pools, and surround ornamental fishponds, swimming pools and water features with wire netting on sturdy posts, otherwise you will find your Labrador enjoying a dip!

The garden shed is usually home to expensive equipment, sharp tools, dangerous chemicals, slug bait, rat poison, weed-killers, paint etc. Make sure that the door can be firmly bolted and is closed at all times.

There are numerous plants that are poisonous to dogs, so you will need to check what is in your garden (a list of poisonous plants is available on the Internet). Ensure that cocoa mulch has never been used anywhere, as it is very poisonous to dogs. Slug pellets are also lethal. Weedkillers on lawns and paths must be dry before your dog walks over the treated area, as the pads of his feet could absorb the poison.

In the home

Decide which rooms in the house your Labrador is going to occupy. A puppy is best kept downstairs in the kitchen/utility room until he is house trained. Upstairs is a no-go area for a puppy. He must not be allowed to climb stairs until he is at least a year old and his bones are mature.

Once you have selected the rooms to be used, put all remaining valuable items up high, out of reach. Keep him away from the computer and its ancillary bits and bobs. Remove mobile phones, spectacle cases and remote controls for TVs, DVDs and videos. Labradors find all these a joy to retrieve and crunch!

In areas where your Lab passes through, make sure there are no accessible electric cables left plugged in and switched on. Clear up abandoned shoes, socks and clothing, which may be lying around the house.

There are a number of plants that are toxic to dogs.

Many a sock has travelled the length of a Labrador's digestive system. This can prove fatal.

Finally, where food is concerned, a reminder that Labradors believe in the 'help yourself' method, having little conscience in this department. Make sure the fridge, pantry door, and kitchen cupboards are all firmly shut and your grocery shopping bags are out of reach.

Buying equipment

You can purchase most equipment you need from your nearest pet store, pet supermarket, or on-line.

Indoor kennel/crate

Your Labrador will love his very own wire-mesh, indoor dog crate, which most of the time will have the door open. The crate is his own private bedroom, a place where he can take all his toys and trophies; somewhere no one else can invade.

The easily-dismantled wire crate has a removable, plastic tray in the base. The smallest size crate for a Labrador is 24 inches by 37 inches by 27 inches (61 x 94 x 69 cm), and the crate usually has two opening doors.

Before you bring your puppy home, you need to decide where to locate the crate. To become well socialized, he will need to live in the hub of the

Shopping for your puppy is all part of the fun of getting ready for your new arrival.

family, not left in an isolated room, far away from all the daily goings-on. The kitchen or utility room are best, with quick access to the back door to aid initial toilet training.

A crate is an invaluable piece of equipment; it will keep your puppy at safe when you cannot supervise him, and it will provide a quiet refuge for both puppy and adult. Never fall into the trap of using the crate as a place of punishment, and never leave your Labrador confined for lengthy periods – except overnight.

Dog bed

These come in a spectacular range of shapes and sizes. Young puppies often test their teeth out on their beds, so do not waste money buying an expensive bed at this stage. For a puppy, use a 24 inches (60 cm) plastic puppy bed, and once he is fully grown, buy him an easily cleaned, adult plastic dog bed. The minimum size needed is 27 by 18 inches (69 x 46 cm).

Bedding

You will need at least three pieces of synthetic fleece bedding so that there is always some available while the rest is in the wash or drying.

Dog bedding should be regularly washed in the washing machine with non-biological powder, as biological powder can cause skin irritation.

Bowls and buckets

A Labrador's favorite trick is to pick up his bowl and wander around with it in his mouth. Therefore, choose unbreakable, stainless steel bowls; fancy crockery bowls do not survive long when dropped on the tiled kitchen floor.

You will need at least three stainless-steel feeding bowls 8- 10 inches (20- 25 cm) in diameter, preferably with cone-shaped sides and non-slip bottom rim. Because of the conical shape, your Labrador is unlikely to pick these bowls up.

A 9 inches (22.5 cm) stainless-steel water pail, which can be sited outdoors during the day (except in frosty weather), is also a good investment.

Collar and lead

An eight-week-old puppy will not have been lead trained. However, when you collect him, take a 15 inches (38 cm) soft, nylon puppy collar and a non-leather lead, just in case you have any problems with the car breaking down during the journey home and you need to take the puppy out of the car for any length of time. He will outgrow this small collar very quickly. Do not buy an expensive leather collar and lead at this stage, as he will probably chew it up.

It is dangerous to leave a collar on a young Labrador while he is running free unsupervised in your own garden. If a sturdy branch of a shrub gets caught through the collar while the puppy is speeding past, it could easily break his neck.

For a well-trained adult Labrador, a rounded leather collar or plain nylon collar, usually around 24-26 inches (60-66 cm) long, and a leather lead are ideal.

Grooming gear

A puppy should get used to being groomed from an early age – even though the Labrador's short coat does not need much attention. Buy a soft brush and spend a few minutes brushing your pup every day so he gets used to being handled in this way.

For information on adult grooming, see page 116.

Toys

From puppyhood through to old age, your Labrador will amuse himself with tennis balls, squeaky toys, rubber rings, plastic dumbbells, rope tugs, kongs, and empty plastic bottles – all are sources of play and enjoyment.

Soft toys are available in plenty from charity shops. Make sure they are safe for very young children, in which case they will suit your dog, otherwise removable parts, such as glass eyes, could be detached and swallowed.

Stairgate

Purchase a stairgate for the bottom of the stairs if your adult Labrador is not to be allowed upstairs. Adult Labradors quickly learn how to open simple catches on stairgates, so purchase one with a flip over, locking catch, operated by depressing two safety buttons.

Settling in

Whether you have decided on an adult Labrador, a rescued dog or a puppy, do not overwhelm him with too many visitors when he first arrives home. He needs to settle in quietly and get his bearings. If the puppy or adult is shy, do not over-face him; leave him be for the time being.

Offer him a drink of water, then show him around the garden and take him to his designated toilet spot. After a while, give him his first dinner. Food is the way to a Labrador's heart. He will probably forget all his apprehension, gobble his dinner, and, from then on, be your best pal – completely won over by your whole family, who deliver such gorgeous meals!

During the changeover period, make sure you stick to the food the breeder has given you, otherwise his tummy may become upset. If you do change the food for whatever reason, take several days to do so, gradually mixing the new food in with the old food.

For information on feeding, see pages 106.

Introduce your puppy to his crate at an early stage. Line it with bedding and put a safe toy inside so it looks inviting. Tempt your puppy to go into the crate with a treat and then stroke him and praise him when he is in there. To begin with, make sure you are in the same room when you shut your puppy in his crate so he does not feel abandoned. Once settled, leave him for short periods. In between times, leave the crate door open so your puppy can come and go as he pleases.

Meeting the family

Children in the family will be very excited by the new arrival, but they should be encouraged to be calm so as not to frighten him. Let them pat and stroke him gently, but no squealing.

A puppy should be held firmly on a parent's lap for the children to stroke. Never allow youngsters to pick up a puppy; he will be too heavy, will wriggle and go crashing to the floor. Make sure the children play with the pup while they are sitting on the floor and not standing up. Make them aware that the puppy has very sharp teeth and scratchy claws and to keep their faces and fingers well away from the puppy.

Do not let children torment the puppy by holding him down and tickling his feet or pulling his ears or tail. If things get too exuberant, put the puppy in his crate for a while with a treat.

Before eating food, after playing with the puppy, ensure the children wash their hands.

Do not let your puppy assume he can climb on to your lap every day by right – he will still want to do it when he is fully grown, which is a rather different prospect...

Below: If early interactions are supervised, your puppy will soon find his place in the family.

Meeting resident pets

When introducing two adult dogs it is better to do this outside in the garden or on neutral territory away from home, so arrange to 'accidentally' meet up on a pleasant walk. With the new Labrador on his lead, make a great fuss of your existing dog as you introduce them. Remember not to make the resident dog jealous; he must receive most of the love and attention plus a few extra treats. They may have the odd grump at each other, but within a couple of weeks, the hierarchy will have been sorted out between them and they should be firm friends. Avoid leaving them together, unattended, before this time.

When introducing a puppy, do not let him make free with the other pet's toys, bed or food, and never leave the puppy with an older dog at this introductory stage. In the early months do not allow the puppy to run freely with adult dogs. They tend to play far too roughly and delight in running puppies down, causing possible bone damage.

The resident cat may or may not take to your new Labrador. The cat will be very aloof initially. Do not leave the new puppy with a cat, as the pup will be inquisitive and is likely to come off worse in any argument. Eyes can be badly damaged, so extra vigilance is needed.

Allow the puppy and older dog to work out their own relationship.

Ensure the cat can keep his dignity and escape out of the way without being chased. You also need to make sure his bed is not taken nor his dinner stolen by the impudent young Labrador. Hopefully, the pair will become great friends.

The first night

During the day, the puppy will have met everyone, eaten, played and, hopefully, toileted outside, so he should be tired by bedtime. Put newspaper at the front of the crate so he does not have to soil his bedding, and settle him in his crate with a cuddly toy (making sure it is 100 per cent safe).a biscuit and a small water bucket clipped to the side of the crate.

A radio turned on low or a loud-ticking alarm-clock may help a puppy to feel that he has not been abandoned; a hot-water bottle or heated pad under his blanket in his bed will also make him relax. After such a busy day, he may drop off to sleep and only wake when you appear at breakfast time. On the other hand, he may howl plaintively non-stop for a few hours. He may feel utterly sad and dejected, lonely and chilly, being on his own for the very first time without his brothers and sisters to keep him snug.

It is very difficult to harden your heart and ignore his cries. Ideally, you should do this, but most owners will end up going down to comfort the sad little fellow, who, in turn, thinks: "Wow, this is great! If I want to see my owner in the middle of the night, all I've got to do is howl a bit louder!"

If you cannot bear the sound of his cries, for this first night only, take his crate upstairs and set it up beside your bed. Carry the puppy upstairs and put him in the crate. He should sleep soundly then. The next night you really must Ignore his cries and make him sleep downstairs on his own. He will soon get used to it.

|House training

This is easy and your puppy will usually get the idea within a few days. The best plan is to allocate a toileting area in your garden and take your puppy to this spot every time he needs to relieve himself.

Establish a routine and make sure you take your puppy out at the following times:

- First thing in the morning.
- After meals.
- On waking.
- Following a play session.
- Last thing at night.

A puppy should be taken out to relieve himself every two hours as an absolute minimum. The more often your puppy gets it 'right', the quicker he will learn to be clean in the house. It helps if you use a verbal cue, such as "Hurry up" or"Busy", when your pup is performing and, in time, this will trigger the desired response.

Do not be tempted to put your puppy out on the doorstep in the hope that he will toilet on his own. Most pups simply sit there, waiting to get back inside the house! No matter how bad the weather is, accompany your puppy and give him lots of praise when he performs correctly.

Do not rush back inside as soon as he has finished. Your puppy might start to delay in the hope of prolonging his time outside with you. Praise him, have a quick game – and then you can both return indoors.

When accidents happen

No matter how vigilant you are, there are bound to be accidents. If you witness the accident, take your puppy outside immediately, and give him lots of praise if he finishes his business out there.

If you are not there when he has an accident, do not scold him when you finally do see what has happened. He will not remember what he has done and will not understand why his lovely owner is so cross.

When you clean up, use a product that breaks down the enzymes in the urine that cause it to smell. If the scent lingers (even if the human owner can't smell it), this can tempt your puppy to use the same spot again. Some dogs are allergic to deodorizing products, so make sure you check the label and try to choose one made with animals in mind.

Take your puppy out at regular intervals and he will soon understand what is required.

Choosing a diet

Labradors will eat anything you choose to feed them. They are not fussy eaters, so there is a great choice open to you with regard to what to purchase.

The selection of dry food from different manufacturers is enormous and this has become the staple diet of the majority of Labradors worldwide. All-in-one complete diets take the guesswork out of feeding, having all the necessary protein, vitamins and minerals added for each life stage. Its crunchiness ensures teeth are always clean and strong, too.

Some breeders still feed tripe and wholemeal biscuit. It smells, but the dogs love it. Tripe can easily cause weight increase if fed too generously. Other dog owners feed minced, cooked beef, which is available to buy frozen in bulk and fed with biscuit.

In this age of questioning processed products and the possibility of health problems they might cause, the BARF diet has evolved. Biologically Appropriate Raw Food is gaining popularity and whole chickens and bones are fed to, and enjoyed by, many dogs.

In the end, as you will soon find out, your Labrador will appreciate whatever food you give him!

Feeding regimes

As Labrador 'clocks' are very accurate, never do anything at exactly the same time each day, otherwise he will expect you to be there, bang on time, every single day. This includes feeding. If you establish a regular set feeding time, exactly five minutes before that time he may annoyingly start to bark. This is to remind you that, in case you had forgotten, dinnertime is fast approaching and you ought to get your skates on! Therefore, I suggest you feed at a slightly different time each day.

Feeding a puppy

When you collect your puppy at eight weeks of age he will be having four regularly spaced meals daily. As he grows, the meals will increase in quantity but decrease in number. Water should always be available.

At about 12 weeks of age, your puppy may start to pick at his fourth meal so this is the time to cut out the final evening meal and increase the amount fed at the other three meals.

When he is about six months of age, the lunchtime meal may be dropped. From then onwards, feed two meals a day, one at breakfast and the other at teatime. Always use the amounts printed on the product bag as a rough guide, but also watch his waistline.

It is important that no supplements are added to an all-in-one balanced food; this could cause bone-growth abnormalities.

Food for adults

Once he is adult, your Labrador's dietary requirements are pretty basic. The Labrador is a good-doer and while he will always heartily appreciate whatever food you put down for him to eat, it is not necessary for you to buy the most expensive brand on the market; a mid-priced one will do very well.

Your Labrador's breeder or rescue charity will have given you details of what food is most suitable. Most proprietary brands of dry dog food are available in a balanced age-specific range: puppy, junior (for growing dogs), adult, senior and working.

Moisten the food with cold water immediately before it is fed, which prevents your Labrador swallowing it too quickly. He will also enjoy a bone-shaped or oval biscuit for breakfast and at bedtime.

As with a puppy, any changes to the diet must be carried out over several days to avoid tummy upsets.

Bones

If you wish to give your Labrador a bone, provide a large, fresh marrowbone (cooked ones splinter and they can swallow the dangerously sharp bits). Scrape most of the very rich marrow fat out of a fresh bone

As your puppy grows, you will need to adjust the amount you are feeding.

with a spoon and give the bone for only around 30 minutes, otherwise he will grind the whole thing up, swallow it all and make himself very sick for the next 24 hours.

Dangers of obesity

Labradors love food. Owners love their Labradors and some express that great love by falling for their Labrador's pleading looks. Unfortunately, if this is not done carefully, treats become excess food and this excess is stored as body fat. A fat Labrador will most likely have health problems and a shorter life than one of the correct weight.

This is not to say that too thin is good, either. Your dog should neither be too fat nor too thin. You should be able to feel each individual rib beneath the skin and flesh covering his ribcage, but you should not be able to see the lines of his ribs – if you can, he is too thin. Another good test to check if he is too fat is to feel his brisket, between his front legs. In a dog of the correct weight, there should be no excess flesh and certainly none hanging down.

Keep a close check on your Labrador's weight to guard against the dangers of obesity.

Caring for your Labrador

The Labrador is such an easy dog to own and care for. With his bright eyes, smiley face, and adorable character, he brings out the very best in everyone he meets. If he comes from health-checked parents, he is likely to be a healthy, sound dog as long as you give him the routine care he needs.

Grooming

The Labrador has the ultimate low maintenance coat. He has a thick, double coat, consisting of a waterproof topcoat, which repels dirt, and a warm, thick undercoat. To keep him healthy and well groomed, a daily brush with a stiff dandy brush will spruce up his coat and remove any dried mud.

Do not try to brush wet mud off the coat; wait until it is dry. You can use a wide-toothed comb and a narrow-toothed comb to remove dead hairs.

After a wet walk, use a towel to dry him off, and, once dry, rub him all over with a piece of kitchen towel to remove grease and dirt and then use a damp wash-leather to make him sparkle.

For the twice-yearly moult, consider buying a shedding rake. The shedding rake must be used very carefully, as it could scratch the skin if used roughly. However, it does work wonderfully well, removing clouds of dead undercoat.

Bathing

The short-coated Labrador rarely needs bathing – unless he has rolled in something obnoxious!

Bear in mind that bathing makes the Labrador's coat very soft for five days. If you intend to show your dog, bath him at least one week before the show so that the coat returns to its normal harsh-to-the-touch texture before the event.

Nail care

Inspect your Labrador's nails on a regular basis to make sure they are not long or curled. This is especially important with older dogs.

Accustom your puppy to being grooming from an early age.

A daily brush will keep the coat in good order.

A rake can be used when the coat is shedding.

You can use a wide toothed or a narrow-toothed comb.

I use guillotine nail clippers, which are ideal for Labrador claws. Make sure you do not cut into the quick – the blood-filled part of the nail – which bleeds profusely if nicked in error. Causing a nail to bleed will hurt your Lab – and the next time he spies you with the nail clippers, he will be off to hide under the table!

If you are worried about trimming your Labrador's nails, you can seek help from your vet or from a professional groomer.

Eye care

Your Labrador's eyes should be clear and bright. A daily wipe of the inner corner with a tissue is all that is required.

Ear inspection

Check your Labrador's ears on a weekly basis to ensure they are clean and odor-free. There are many proprietary ear cleaners and ear wipes available from pet stores. However, I believe the less you put down the dog's ears, the better. A weekly wipe with a tissue or moist cotton wool (cotton) should suffice to remove any dirt. Do not poke cotton-buds down the dog's ears as you could inflict damage.

A daily wipe with a moist tissue will keep eyes free from debris.

Clean the ears but do not probe too deeply into the ear canal.

If you feed a soft diet, you will need to clean teeth on a regular basis.

Nails will need trimming, including the dewclaw – the dog's 'thumb'.

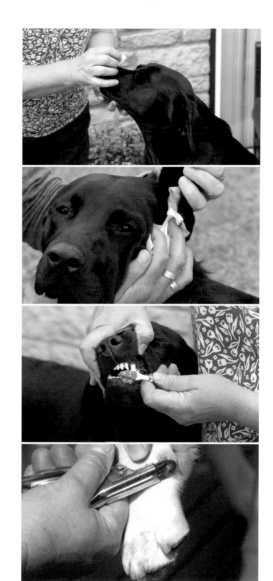

Dental care

Eating dried food and gnawing bones aids tooth cleansing, preventing the build up of tartar. If you decide to feed a softer diet, you will probably need to attend to your Labrador's teeth more often. If you need to clean his teeth, doggy toothpaste and finger-worn doggy toothbrushes are available at pet stores.

Exercise guidelines

Although you will be looking forward to taking your Labrador out for walks, you need to be very careful about exercising a young puppy. Growing bones do not calcify until a puppy is around 12 months of age. It cannot be emphasized too strongly that if a puppy is over-exercised before that time, permanent damage could be done to the skeletal frame, possibly harming the hips, hocks or elbows. This type of injury means that your Lab may well become arthritic in later life.

Up to six months of age, a youngster needs very little exercise apart from a run around your well-fenced garden. You should also avoid any type of rough play. Although he will naturally retrieve, do not be tempted to throw things too far for him.

From 6 to 12 months of age, your Labrador can gradually be given more gentle exercise on the lead, aiming for two miles daily at 12 months.

From 12 to 18 months, exercise can be increased until you can take your Labrador wherever you wish to go – short walks or long walks – for the rest of his life.

Exercise should be limited during the vulnerable growing period.

Adult Labradors love to play for hours on end and will happily retrieve anything you care to throw. Old tennis balls are ideal, but never throw sticks or stones, as the former can damage the back of the dog's throat and the latter may break his teeth or be swallowed.

It is not a good ideal to allow your Lab to play with a football. He will career around so roughly with it that he could end up lame or with damaged toes.

If you are buying a rubber ball, ensure there is either no hole in it, or that there are at least two holes in it to prevent a vacuum forming should the dog's tongue gets stuck through the hole. There have been dreadful accidents with Labs getting their tongues stuck in the single hole and subsequently requiring drastic veterinary treatment.

The older Labrador

Labradors are classed as veterans in the show ring from the age of seven. However, most will still be very sprightly until well past 10 years. As a Labrador approaches his teen years, he will still enjoy his daily walk, but may become a little slower. On his return home will seek his warm, comfortable bed in which to doze away the rest of the day, before his still eagerly-awaited evening meal.

With his exercise reduced, watch your Labrador's waistline. Be prepared to cut his nails, including dewclaws, frequently as, with less exercise, they will wear more slowly.

Labradors, just like humans, can have strokes, which at first may look fatal but which often are not. Do not be too hasty. Just because your dog has had a stroke doesn't necessarily mean he has to be put down on the day of the stroke. If he regains consciousness, even though he is walking beside a wall at a peculiar angle, wait a few days; quite often he will have revived completely by the end of this time. He may live many months or even years longer.

The older Labrador often grows the odd fatty tumor somewhere, usually on his side. They are large, hard, round lumps growing directly under the skin or muscle, up to the size of half a grapefruit.

You need to be aware of the changing needs of your Labrador as he grows older.

Do not be alarmed: although they may look rather odd, they usually prove non-malignant. As long as the lumps do not impair the dog's mobility, they are best left alone.

Old age often brings with it the same problems applicable to dogs as to humans: deafness, sore gums, rotting or worn teeth, failing eyesight, sore feet, tender limbs and an intolerance of youngsters! Keep his ears and eyes clean and check his teeth. Be sympathetic with him and make his last few years comfortable.

Eventually, the day will come when you have to steel yourself to say a final goodbye to your dear old Labrador. Perhaps he is in constant pain; maybe he refuses his food; his hind legs have become unable to support him, or he is totally incontinent, something he will hate. However many Labradors you own, the final deed will break your heart, but you must put your dog first and allow him to leave this life with dignity and suffering as little pain as possible. When you feel the time has come, discuss the matter with your vet and allow him to make the final decision.

The sure signs of decline in a Labrador are:-

- Disinclination to eat or unable to eat or drink without being sick

- Incontinent and unable to raise himself to go outside to the toilet.

- Unable to raise himself off his bed to walk about or back legs unable to support him.

- Chronically lame/medication unable to ease pain.

- Inoperable tumors, causing chronic pain and impeding the function of limbs or organs.

- Unable to breathe without coughing.

- Crying helplessly, with a worn-out, pleading look, to stop the pain and misery he is going through.

More than likely throughout his happy life with you, he will never have experienced anything unpleasant, certainly not discomfort or unbearable pain. You must be very brave, for he has loved you faithfully every day of his life and now, in his time of need, you are the only one who can help relieve him from further suffering.

When the day comes, you must put your emotions aside. Face up to your duty and send for the vet to come to your home and put your dear old friend peacefully to sleep in his home surroundings. This is so much better than taking him on a final, uncomfortable car journey to the vet's busy surgery.

At home, in his own comfy dog bed, he is resting, quiet and relaxed, under no stress. The vet will greet him kindly and will probably receive a heart-wrenching, trusty wag, which makes the situation even harder to bear. I kneel down and gently stroke my dear Lab's lovely face, give his ears a final gentle caress, and tell him all is well and what a good dog he is. Although inwardly I am torn apart with grief, I must not allow myself to appear distressed, otherwise he will be alarmed. I want his passing to be calm and peaceful.

The final injection is quietly and painlessly given; the deed is done, kindly and quickly with no stress. Within just a few seconds my dear old pal is fast asleep; gone forever, but free at last from pain and discomfort. I am in pieces and am allowed to show it! Just like me, when you have to say a final goodbye to your dear old Labrador, you and your family will cry your hearts out and grieve for many days. This is quite normal, but always remember that your selfless gift has freed him from further pain.

If wished, your vet will arrange your dog's cremation at a pet crematorium. A few days later, his ashes will be tastefully returned to you in an urn, to be buried in the garden where he played so happily throughout his life.

You will never forget your Labrador and swear you will never replace him. However, with time you may find another bright Labrador will come merrily bouncing through the doorway, to join your family and creep into your heart once again. The fond memories of your faithful friend will never fade and the joy of watching the antics of the newcomer will surely bring happy memories of the past to the fore, as the cycle of life continues.

Training guidelines

When you are training it will help to have some guidelines which will increase your chances of success.

- Find a reward your Labrador really wants. This could be a toy but, with most Labradors, a tasty food treat is the key to success. You can vary the reward so you have high value treats (cheese or sausage) for teaching new exercises and recalls away from home, and low value treats (dry kibble) for routine training.

- Work on your tone of voice. This will be far more meaningful to your Labrador than the words you are saying. Use a bright, happy, upbeat tone when you are training, and a deep, firm voice when you catch him red handed – raiding the bin, for example. Go over the top when praising your Labrador so that he understands how pleased you are with him.

- Train in short sessions. This applies particularly to puppies, who have a very short attention span, but adults will also switch off if sessions are too long. Remember, it is the quality of work you are after – not the quantity.

- Never train if you are preoccupied or if you are in a bad mood. Your Labrador will pick up on your negative vibes, and the session is doomed to disaster.

- Teach one lesson at a time and only proceed to the next lesson when the first has been mastered.

- Praise success lavishly so your Labrador understands that you are really pleased with him. Tell him how clever he is, stroke him, and reward him with a toy or a treat.

- Make sure training sessions always end on a positive note – even if this means abandoning an exercise for the time being and finishing with something you know your Labrador can do.

- Above all, make sure your training sessions are fun, with lots of play and plenty of opportunities to reward you dog, so that you both enjoy spending time together.

- Never reprimand your Labrador for getting it wrong – he may well be uncertain about what you are asking rather than being deliberately naughty. If your Lab makes a mistake, simply ignore it and ask him to " try again". When he does get it right, praise him to the skies.

Below: Make sure training sessions are positive and enjoyable for both you and your Labrador.

IFirst lessons

A Labrador puppy's brain is like a blank canvas. It pays to commence training from the very first moment he comes to live with you at two months of age. At this time of his life, more than any other, the blank canvas is far more easily filled.

Wearing a collar

- When you first bring your puppy home and have got to know each other, accustom him to wearing a soft puppy collar for a few minutes. Fit the collar so that you can get at least two fingers between the collar and his neck. Then have a game to distract his attention. This will work for a few moments; then he will stop, put his back leg up behind his neck and scratch away at the peculiar itchy thing round his neck, which feels so odd.

- Bend down, rotate the collar, pat him on the head and distract him by gently throwing a toy for him to retrieve. Once he has worn the collar for a

few minutes each day, he will soon ignore it and become used to it.

- Remember, never leave the collar on the puppy unsupervised, especially when he is outside in the garden.

Walking on a lead

- Once your puppy is used to the collar, take him outside into your secure garden where there are no distractions.

- Attach the lead and, to begin with, allow him to wander with the lead kept lose so that the puppy doesn't feel as though he has it on. Follow the pup where he wants to go. Then increase the tension on the lead, taking care not to pull, so that your pup gets used to the sensation of being attached to you.

- The next stage is to get your Labrador to follow you, and for this you will need some tasty treats. Show him a treat in your hand, and encourage him to follow you. Walk a few paces, and if he is co-operating, stop and reward him. If he puts on the brakes, simply change direction and lure him with the treat – it does not take a Labrador long to realize that if he co-operates, a treat will follow.

- Now introduce some changes of direction so your puppy is walking confidently alongside you. At this stage, introduce a verbal cue "Heel" when your puppy is in the correct position. You can then graduate to excursions outside the home – as long as he has completed his vaccination programme. Before the age of 6 months, make sure these are for socialization and training only. Take care not to over-exercise your puppy. Start in quiet areas and build up to busier environments.

- If your puppy tries to pull on the lead, do not try to pull him back into position – he will think this is all part of a game. Simply come to a halt, tell your puppy to "Heel" and then move forward again, rewarding him when he is in the correct position. If he persists in pulling, stop, and walk in the opposite direction. Your Labrador needs to learn pulling gets him nowhere – he only makes progress when he walking on a loose lead.

The aim is for your Labrador to walk on a loose lead, neither pulling ahead nor lagging behind.

Come when called

Teaching a reliable recall is invaluable for both you and your Labrador. You are secure in the knowledge that he will come back when he is called, and your Lab benefits from being allowed free running exercise.

Your puppy may have learnt to "Come" in the confined space of your kitchen – and this is a good place to build up a positive association with the verbal cue – particularly if you ask your puppy to "Come" to get his dinner!

The next stage is to transfer the lesson to the garden. Arm yourself with some treats, and wait until your puppy is distracted. Then call him, using a higher-pitched, excited tone of voice. If your puppy responds, immediately reward him with a treat. If he is slow to come, run away a few steps and then call again, making yourself sound really exciting.

Jump up and down, open your arms wide to welcome him; it doesn't matter how silly you look, he needs to see you as the most fun person in the world.

Now you are ready to introduce some distractions. Try calling him when someone else is in the garden, or wait a few minutes until he is investigating a really interesting scent. When he responds, make a really big fuss of him and give him some extra treats so he knows it is worth his while to come to you.

When you have an extremely reliable recall in the garden and your pup is mature enough, you can venture into the outside world. However, be very careful as you do not want to lose your puppy. Do not be too ambitious to begin with; try a recall in a quiet place with the minimum of distractions and only progress to more challenging environments if your Labrador is responding well.

Do not make the mistake of asking your dog to come only at the end of a walk. What is the incentive in coming back to you if all you do is clip on his lead and head for home? Instead, call your dog at random times throughout the walk, giving him a treat and a stroke, and then letting him go free again. In this way, coming to you is always rewarding, and does not signal the end of his free run.

Coming when called should always be seen as a fun option – so be ready with praise and rewards when your Labrador responds.

Stationary exercises

The Sit and Down commands are not difficult to teach if you are using positive rewards; even a very young puppy is capable of understanding. Work on these before progressing to the Stay exercise.

Sit: step by step

The best method is to lure your Labrador into position, and for this you can use a treat, a toy, or his food bowl.

- Hold the reward above your Labrador's head. As he looks up, he will lower his hindquarters and go into a sit.

- Practice this a few times and when your puppy understands what you are asking, introduce the verbal cue "Sit".

Down: step by step

These are the commands to get your dog lying flat on the floor and can be taught indoors or out. Either word may be used.

- With your dog on the lead and in the Sit position on your left-hand side, kneel down with your knee on the end of his lead so he cannot run off.

- Show your dog you are holding a treat in your right hand and make sure his attention is on you (or rather your hand).

- Close your fist around the treat and move your hand towards the floor between your dog's front legs.

- As you do this, give the command "Down".

- Being a typical, hungry Labrador, your dog's nose will follow the treat in your hand down to the floor.

- Gradually move the treat forward and his body will be horizontal in the Down position.

- Once your Lab is in the correct position, give him the treat and praise him lavishly.

- Repeat the exercise frequently. Gradually, as he learns this command, you can perfect the straightness of his position.

Labradors learn so quickly and love pleasing you. You will be thrilled and impressed with the results of your training skills.

Control exercises

Teaching your Labrador to Wait and Stay is not the most exciting task, but they introduce control which will help to keep your Labrador safe in all situations.

Wait

This exercise teaches your Labrador to "Wait" in position until you give the next command; it differs from the Stay exercise where your Labrador must stay where you have left him for a more prolonged period.

The most useful application of "Wait" is when you are getting your dog out of the car and you need him to stay in position until you clip on his lead.

Start with your puppy on the lead to give you a greater chance of success. Ask him to "Sit" and stand in front him. Step back one pace, holding your hand, palm flat, facing him. Wait a second and then come back to stand in front of him.

You can reward this response and release your dog with a word, such as "OK". Practice a few times, gradually increasing the distance and the time you can leave your Labrador, and then introduce the verbal cue "Wait".

You can reinforce the lesson by using it in different situations, such as asking your Labrador to "Wait" before you put his food bowl down.

Stay

You need to differentiate this exercise by using a different hand signal and a different verbal cue.

Start by telling your puppy to "Sit" facing you while on a loose lead. Take a step backwards and raise your right hand, like a policeman. Give the command "Stay" and take another step backwards. If he moves or tries to wander off, quietly correct him – "No. Stay" – and put him back in position. Repeat the exercise until he gets it right.

Vary the exercise by moving backwards or out to either side of your puppy. If he stays correctly, walk back to him and praise him. Eventually, try walking in a circle around him. He will learn to watch you and "Stay", without moving. Give him lots of praise. Once you think he is steady, try the lesson without the lead.

The ideal owner

An ideal Labrador owner is someone who has time to spend with their dog each day. Someone who is at home – an owner who can enjoy every minute of Labrador companionship and devotion.

Of course, this ideal is rarely possible these days and Labradors find excellent homes with those who manage to be at home at some time during the day. It could be someone who works mornings only, or is able to come back at lunchtime to go for a 30-minute walk. Some owners work from home and some people are able to take the dog to work, as long as he does not have to be left in the car for any length of time.

The main requirement is that a Labrador should never be abandoned all day long. He needs human contact, mental stimulation and exercise.

A Labrador also needs to learn his place in the family pack. He needs to understand where his boundaries lie and respect his fellow pack members, young and old alike. As an owner you must establish this relationship with firmness, fairness and consistency so your Lab always knows what is being asked of him and is happy to accept your leadership

Opportunities for Labradors

If you are enjoying training your Labrador, you may want to get involved in more advanced training, or take part in one of the many canine sports on offer.

Good Citizen Scheme

The Good Citizen Scheme is run by the national Kennel Clubs in both the UK and the USA, and is designed to promote responsible ownership and to teach basic obedience and good manners so your dog is a model citizen in the community. In the UK there are four award levels: Puppy Foundation, Bronze, Silver and Gold. In the US there is one test.

The show ring

If you intend to show your puppy, you will need to attend ringcraft classes so you train your dog to perform in the ring and you can also learn about show ring etiquette.

When your Labrador has learnt how to behave in the show ring, you are ready to compete. The first classes are for puppies from six months of age and progress through different categories depending on the type of show, which can range from. informal fun day events to the all-important Championship shows where Labradors compete for the prestigious title of Show Champion, or, even better, Champion, if they already hold a Show Gundog Working Certificate.

Showing is great fun, but at the top level it is highly competitive, so you will need to learn the art of winning – and losing – graciously.

Agility

This is great fun to watch and join in. Against the clock, at the fastest speed they can muster, dogs jump over obstacles, through tires and tunnels, and negotiate the contact equipment, which includes an A-frame, a dog walk and a seesaw. While the Labrador will enjoy agility, he is not the speediest. However, with training, he will become a reliable competitor and you will both get a lot of fun from taking part.

Your Labrador cannot begin Agility training until he is fully grown, as his joints are vulnerable to damage while he still growing.

Both you and your Labrador need to be fit to compete in agility.

Obedience

Competitive obedience exercises include: heelwork at varying paces with dog and handler following a pattern decided by the judge, stays, recalls, retrieves, sendaways, scent discrimination and distance control. The exercises get progressively harder as you rise up the classes. A Labrador will readily learn these exercises, but, at the top level a very high degree of precision and accuracy is called for.

Field Trials

These are highly competitive, sometimes arduous, events over rough territory, held under Kennel Club rules to resemble a day's shooting in the field. Field trial Labradors will be from a working background as opposed to showing, and are expected to work with all manner of game, from rabbits and hares, to partridges and pheasants.

Tracking

The Labrador, with his outstanding sense of smell, is a good choice for this demanding sport where the dog must learn to follow scent trails of varying age, over different types of terrain. In the UK tracking is incorporated into Working Trials where a dog must also compete in two other elements (control and agility), but in the US it is a sport in its own right,

Health care for Labradors

We are fortunate that the Labrador is a healthy dog, with no exaggerations, and with good routine care, a well balanced diet, and sufficient exercise, most dogs will experience few health problems.

However, it is your responsibility to put a programme of preventative health care in place – and this should start from the moment your puppy, or older dog, arrives in his new home.

Vaccinations

Dogs are subject to a number of contagious diseases. In the old days, these were killers, and resulted in heartbreak for many owners. Vaccinations have now been developed, and the occurrence of the major infectious diseases is now very rare. However, this will only remain the case if all pet owners follow a strict policy of vaccinating their dogs.

There are vaccinations available for the following diseases:

Adenovirus: This affects the liver; affected dogs have a classic 'blue eye'.

Distemper: A viral disease which causes chest and gastro-intestinal damage. The brain may also be affected, leading to fits and paralysis.

Parvovirus: This causes severe gastro enteritis, and most commonly affects puppies.

Leptospirosis: This bacterial disease is carried by rats and affects many mammals, including humans. It causes liver and kidney damage.

Rabies: A virus that affects the nervous system and is invariably fatal. The first signs are abnormal behavior when the infected dog may bite another animal or a person. Paralysis and death follow. Vaccination is compulsory in most countries. In the UK, dogs travelling overseas must be vaccinated.

Kennel Cough: There are several strains of Kennel Cough, but they all result in a harsh, dry, cough. This disease is rarely fatal; in fact most dogs make a good recovery within a matter of weeks and show few signs of ill health while they are affected. However, kennel cough is highly infectious among dogs that live together so, for this reason, most boarding kennels will insist that your dog is protected by the vaccine, which is given as nose drops.

Lyme Disease: This is a bacterial disease transmitted by ticks (see page 166). The first signs are limping, but the heart, kidneys and nervous system can also be affected. The ticks that transmit the disease occur in specific regions, such as the north-east states of the USA, some of the southern states, California and the upper Mississippi region. Lyme disease is till rare in the UK so vaccinations are not routinely offered.

Vaccination program

In the UK, vaccinations are routinely given for distemper, adenovirus, leptospirosis and parvovirus.

In the USA, the American Animal Hospital Association advises vaccination for core diseases, which they list as: distemper, adenovirus, parvovirus and rabies. The requirement for vaccinating for non-core diseases – leptospriosis, Lyme disease and kennel cough – should be assessed depending on a dog's individual risk and his likely exposure to the disease.

In most cases, a puppy will start his vaccinations at around eight weeks of age, with the second part given in a fortnight's time. However, this does vary depending on the individual policy of veterinary practices, and the incidence of disease in your area.

You should also talk to your vet about whether to give annual booster vaccinations. This depends on an individual dog's levels of immunity, and how long a particular vaccine remains effective.

Parasites

No matter how well you look after your Labrador, you will have to accept that parasites – internal and external – are ever present, and you need to take preventative action.

Internal parasites: As the name suggests, these parasites live inside your dog. Most will find a home in the digestive tract, but there is also a parasite that lives in the heart. If infestation is unchecked, a dog's health will be severely jeopardized, but routine preventative treatment is simple and effective.

External parasites: These parasites live on your dog's body – in his skin and fur, and sometimes in his ears.

Roundworm

This is found in the small intestine, and signs of infestation will be a poor coat, a pot belly, diarrhoea and lethargy. Pregnant mothers should be treated, but it is almost inevitable that roundworms will be passed on to the puppies. For this reason, a breeder will start a worming programme, which you will need to continue. Ask your vet for advice on treatment, which will need to continue throughout your dog's life.

Tapeworm

Infection occurs when fleas and lice are ingested; the adult worm takes up residence in the small intestine, releasing mobile segments (which contain eggs) which can be seen in a dog's feces as small rice-like grains. The only other obvious sign of infestation is irritation of the anus. Again, routine preventative treatment is required throughout your Labrador's life.

Heartworm

This parasite is transmitted by mosquitoes, so it is more likely to be present in areas with a warm, humid climate. It is found throughout the USA, although its prevalence does vary, but is rarely seen in the UK at present.

Heartworms live in the right side of the heart and larvae can grow up to 14 inches (35 cm) in length. A dog with heartworm is at severe risk from heart failure, so preventative treatment, as advised by your vet, is essential. Dogs living in the USA should also have regular tests to check for infection.

Lungworm

Lungworm, or Angiostrongylus vasorum, is a parasite that lives in the heart and major blood vessels supplying the lungs. It can cause many problems, such as breathing difficulties, excessive bleeding, sickness and diarrhoea, seizures, and can even be fatal. The parasite is carried by slugs and snails, and the dog becomes infected when ingesting these, often accidentally when rummaging through undergrowth. Lungworm is not common, but it is on the increase and a responsible owner should be aware of it. Fortunately, it is easily preventable and even affected dogs usually make a full recovery if treated early enough. Your vet will be able to advise you on the risks in your area and what form of treatment may be required.

Routine preventative treatment for external parasites will be needed throughout your dog's life.

Fleas

A dog may carry dog fleas, cat fleas, and even human fleas. The flea stays on the dog only long enough to have a blood meal and to breed, but its presence will result in itching and scratching. If your dog has an allergy to fleas – which is usually a reaction to the flea's saliva – he will scratch himself until he is raw.

Spot-on treatment, which should be administered on a routine basis, is easy to use and highly effective on all types of fleas. You can also treat your dog with a spray or with insecticidal shampoo. Bear in mind that the whole environment your dog lives in will need to be sprayed, and all other pets living in your home will also need to be treated.

How to detect fleas

You may suspect your dog has fleas, but how can you be sure? There are two methods to try.

Run a fine comb through your dog's coat, and see if you can detect the presence of fleas on the skin, or clinging to the comb. Alternatively, sit your dog on some white paper and rub his back. This will dislodge feces from the fleas, which will be visible as small brown specks. To double check, shake the specks on to some damp cotton wool (cotton). Flea feces consists of the dried blood taken from the host, so if the specks turn a lighter shade of red, you know your dog has fleas.

Ticks

These are blood-sucking parasites which are most frequently found in rural area where sheep or deer are present. The main danger is their ability to pass Lyme disease to both dogs and humans. Lyme disease is prevalent in some areas of the USA (see page 159), although it is still rare in the UK. Discuss the local risk and treatment options with your vet.

How to remove a tick

If you spot a tick on your dog, do not try to pluck it off as you risk leaving the hard mouth parts embedded in his skin. The best way to remove a tick is to use a fine pair of tweezers or you can buy a tick remover. Grasp the tick head firmly and then pull the tick straight out from the skin. If you are using a tick remover, check the instructions, as some recommend a circular twist when pulling. When you have removed the tick, clean the area with mild soap and water.

Ear mites

These parasites live in the outer ear canal. The signs of infestation are a brown, waxy discharge, and your dog will continually shake his head and scratch his ear. If you suspect ear mites, a visit to the vet will be needed so that medicated ear drops can be prescribed.

Fur mites

These small, white parasites are visible to the naked eye and are often referred to as 'walking dandruff'.

They cause a scurfy coat and mild itchiness. However, they are zoonotic – transferable to humans – so prompt treatment with an insecticide prescribed by your vet is essential.

Harvest mites

These are picked up from the undergrowth, and can be seen as a bright orange patch on the webbing between the toes, although this can also be found elsewhere on the body, such as on the ear flaps. Treatment is effective with the appropriate insecticide.

Skin mites

There are two types of parasite that burrow into a dog's skin. Demodex canis is transferred from a mother to her pups while they are feeding. Treatment is with a topical preparation, and sometimes antibiotics are needed.

The other skin mite is sarcoptes scabiei, which causes intense itching and hair loss. It is highly contagious, so all dogs in a household will need to be treated, which involves repeated bathing with a medicated shampoo.

Common ailments

As with all living animals, dogs can be affected by a variety of ailments, most of which can be treated effectively after consulting with your vet, who will prescribe appropriate medication and will advise you on how to care for your dog's needs.

Here are some of the more common problems that could affect your Labrador, with advice on how to deal with them.

Anal glands

These are two small sacs on either side of the anus, which produce a dark-brown secretion that dogs use when they mark their territory. The anal glands should empty every time a dog defecates but, if they become blocked or impacted, a dog will experience increasing discomfort.

He may nibble at his rear end, or 'scoot' his bottom along the ground to relieve the irritation. Treatment involves a trip to the vet where the vet will empty the glands manually. It is important to do this without delay or infection may occur.

Dental problems

Good dental hygiene will do much to minimize problems with gum infection and tooth decay. If tartar accumulates to the extent that you cannot remove it by brushing, the vet will need to intervene. In a situation such as this, an anesthetic will need to be administered so the tartar can be removed manually.

Diarrhoea

There are many reasons why a dog has diarrhoea, but most commonly it is the result of scavenging, a sudden change of diet, or an adverse reaction to a particular type of food. The ever-hungry Labrador will eat virtually anything he comes across, and although he has a tough constitution, digestive upset caused by scavenging is not unusual.

If your dog is suffering from diarrhoea, the first step is to withdraw food for a day. It is important that he does not dehydrate, so make sure that fresh drinking water is available. However, drinking too much can increase the diarrhoea, which may be accompanied with vomiting, so limit how much he drinks at any one time.

After allowing the stomach to rest, feed a bland diet, such as white fish or chicken with boiled rice for a few days. In most cases, your dog's motions will return to normal and you can resume your usual feeding regime, although this should be done gradually.

However, if this fails to work and the diarrhoea persists for more than a few days, you should consult you vet. Your dog may have an infection, which needs to be treated with antibiotics, or the diarrhoea may indicate some other problem which needs expert diagnosis.

Ear infections

The Labrador's ears lie close to his head so air cannot circulate as freely as it would in a dog with semi-pricked or pricked ears. Therefore, it is important to keep a close check on your Labrador's ears.

A healthy ear is clean with no sign of redness or inflammation, and no evidence of a waxy brown discharge or a foul odor. If you see your dog scratching his ear, shaking his head, or holding one ear at an odd angle, you will need to consult your vet.

The most likely causes are ear mites (see page 168), an infection, or there may a foreign body, such as a grass seed, trapped in the ear.

Depending on the cause, treatment is with medicated ear drops, possibly containing antibiotics. If a foreign body is suspected, the vet will need to carry our further investigations.

Eye problems

The Labrador's eyes are set square in his skull; they do not protrude, as in breeds like the Pug, so they are not vulnerable to injury.

However, if your Lab's eyes look red and sore, he may be suffering from Conjunctivitis. This may, or may not be accompanied with a watery or a crusty discharge. Conjunctivitis can be caused by a bacterial or viral infection, it could be the result of an injury, or it could be an adverse reaction to pollen.

You will need to consult your vet for a correct diagnosis, but in the case of an infection, treatment with medicated eye drops is effective.

Conjunctivitis may also be the first sign of more serious inherited eye problems, see page 186.

Foreign bodies

In the home, puppies – and some older dogs – cannot resist chewing anything that looks interesting. This is most particularly true of the Labrador who will always be checking for anything that may be edible.

The toys you choose for your dog should be suitably robust to withstand damage, but children's toys can be irresistible. Some dogs will chew – and swallow – anything from socks, tights, and other items from the laundry basket, to golf balls and stones from the garden. Obviously, these items are indigestible and could cause an obstruction in your dog's intestine, which is potentially lethal.

The signs to look for are vomiting, and a tucked up posture. The dog will often be restless and will look as though he is in pain. In this situation, you must get your dog to the vet without delay as surgery will be needed to remove the obstruction.

The other type of foreign body that may cause problems is grass seed. A grass seed can enter an orifice such as a nostril, down an ear, the gap between the eye and the eyelid, or penetrate the soft skin between the toes. It can also be swallowed.

The introduction of a foreign body induces a variety of symptoms, depending on the point of entry and where it travels to. The signs to look for include head

shaking/ear scratching, the eruption of an abscess, sore, inflamed eyes, or a persistent cough. The vet will be able to make a proper diagnosis, and surgery may be required.

Heatstroke

The Labrador is a hardy breed but care should be taken on hot days as heatstroke is a potential danger. When the temperature rises, make sure your dog always has access to shady areas, and wait for a cooler part of the day before going for a walk. Be extra careful if you leave your Labrador in the car, as the temperature can rise dramatically – even on a cloudy day. Heatstroke can happen very rapidly, and unless you are able lower your dog's temperature, it can be fatal.

If your Labrador appears to be suffering from heatstroke, lie him flat and then work at lowering his temperature, covering him with wet towels. As soon as he has made some recovery, take him to the vet where cold intravenous fluids can be administered.

Lameness/limping

There are a wide variety of reasons why a dog can go lame, from a simple muscle strain to a fracture, ligament damage, or more complex problems with

the joints which may be an inherited disorder (see pages 182-188). It takes an expert to make a correct diagnosis, so if you are concerned about your dog, do not delay in seeking help.

As your Labrador becomes elderly, he may suffer from arthritis, which you will see as general stiffness, particularly when he gets up after resting. It will help if you ensure his bed is in a warm, draught-free location, and, if your Lab gets wet after exercise, you must dry him thoroughly.

If your elderly Labrador seems to be in pain, consult your vet who will be able to help with pain relief medication.

Skin problems

If your dog is scratching or nibbling at his skin, the first thing to check for is fleas (see page 165). There are other external parasites which cause itching and hair loss, but you will need a vet to help you find the culprit.

An allergic reaction is another major cause of skin problems. It can be quite an undertaking to find the cause of the allergy, and you will need to follow your vet's advice, which often requires eliminating specific ingredients from the diet, as well as looking at environmental factors.

Inherited & breed-disposed disorders

The Labrador does have a few breed-related disorders, and if diagnosed with any of the diseases listed below, it is important to remember that they can affect offspring so breeding from affected dogs should be discouraged.

There are now recognized screening tests to enable breeders to check for affected individuals and hence reduce the prevalence of these diseases within the breed.

For details of the organizations concerned, see page 186.

DNA testing is also becoming more widely available, and as research into the different genetic diseases progresses, more DNA tests are being developed.

Dead tail

Labradors suffer from a condition known as 'dead tail', 'cold tail' or 'limber tail'. This is most often seen in working breeds and may have some connection with swimming in cold water (potentially just a bath) or a strenuous day's working, although the exact cause is unknown. Ensuring the tail is dried thoroughly, especially at the base, after becoming wet will help prevent dead tail from occurring.

The tail is seen to hang limply from the base, or just below, and may be painful to touch. Rest is the main form of treatment with recovery usually seen within a week or so. Anti-inflammatory preparations may help with the pain and inflammation of the muscles. If there is no improvement then a visit to the vet is necessary, as there may be a further underlying cause of the limp tail, such as fracture or nerve damage.

Elbow dysplasia (ED)

This is a developmental disease where the elbow does not mature correctly and signs of lameness are usually seen in younger, large-breed dogs. Labradors have a high incidence of ED, and so it is essential that all breeding stock is tested. In the UK X-rays are sent to the British Veterinary

Association where a panel will grade each elbow.
In the US, X-rays are submitted to the Orthopedic
Foundation for Animals. Severely affected dogs should
not be bred from.

Surgery may be indicated to correct the
abnormalities, but the affected joints will be more
prone to arthritis later in life.

Exercise-induced collapse

There is an inherited condition in Labradors where
occasional exercise intolerance and collapse may be
seen with strenuous exercise. Initial clinical signs
may be seen in otherwise fit and healthy, generally
over-excitable dogs between five months and five
years. There is no definitive treatment and it is
not usually fatal unless the dog is over-exercised.
Affected individuals, identified by a DNA test, should
not be bred from.

Eye disorders

Labradors can be affected by a number of eye
disorders. Testing is carried out in the UK as part
of a combined scheme run by the British Veterinary
Association, the Kennel Club and the International
Sheep Dog Society. In the US testing is done by the
Canine Eye Registration Foundation.

Generalized progressive retinal atrophy (GPRA)

GPRA is a bilateral degenerative disease of the cells (rods and cones) of the retina, leading initially to night blindness and progressing to complete loss of vision. Dogs are affected from three to four years of age or as late as 10 years. There is no cure. However, there is a DNA test available for younger dogs, before being used for breeding, to prevent carrier individuals passing on the genetic defect.

Hereditary cataracts

Cataracts are an opacification of the lens that tends to occur in older dogs. Labradors suffer from hereditary cataracts where the lens is often affected in younger dogs but may be seen later in life.

There are varying degrees of severity, the inherited form often having little effect on eyesight but, if necessary, surgery is usually successful to treat.

Retinal dysplasia

When the retina develops incorrectly, this may cause impaired vision and blindness depending on the degree of dysplasia and even detachment of the retina from the back of the eye. There are several forms of the disease that Labradors suffer from, varying in severity.

Hip dysplasia (HD)

This is where the ball-and-socket joint of the hip develops incorrectly so that the head of the femur (ball) and the acetabulum of the pelvis (socket) do not fit snugly. This causes pain in the joint and may be seen as lameness in dogs as young as five months old with deterioration into severe arthritis over time. In the US, hip scoring is carried out by the Orthopedic Foundation for Animals. X-rays are submitted when a dog is two years old, categorized as Normal (Excellent, Good, Fair), Borderline, and Dysplastic (Mild, Moderate, Severe). The hip grades of Excellent, Good and Fair are within normal limits and are given OFA numbers.

In the UK, the minimum age for the hips to be assessed by X-ray is 12 months. Each hip can score from a possible perfect 0 to a deformed 53. Both left and right scores are added together to give the total hip score.

Careful and responsible breeding over the years has reduced the prevalence of this disease in Labradors, but care must be taken to ensure that this continues into the future.

Summing up

It may give the pet owner cause for concern to find about health problems that may affect their dog. But it is important to bear in mind that acquiring some basic knowledge is an asset, as it will allow you to spot signs of trouble at an early stage. Early diagnosis is very often the means to the most effective treatment.

Fortunately, the Labrador is a generally healthy and disease-free dog with his only visits to the vet being annual check-ups. In most cases, owners can look forward to enjoying many happy years with this loyal companion.

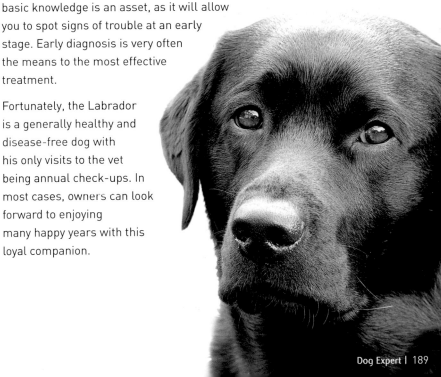

|Useful addresses

Kennel Clubs
Please contact your Kennel Club to obtain contact information about breed clubs in your area.

UK
The Kennel Club (UK)
1 Clarges Street London, W1J 8AB
Telephone: 0870 606 6750
Fax: 0207 518 1058
Web: www.thekennelclub.org.uk

USA
American Kennel Club (AKC)
5580 Centerview Drive, Raleigh, NC 27606.
Telephone: 919 233 9767
Fax: 919 233 3627
Email: info@akc.org
Web: www.akc.org

United Kennel Club (UKC)
100 E Kilgore Rd, Kalamazoo,
MI 49002-5584, USA.
Tel: 269 343 9020
Fax: 269 343 7037
Web: www.ukcdogs.com

Australia
Australian National Kennel Council (ANKC)
The Australian National Kennel Council is the administrative body for pure breed canine affairs in Australia. It does not, however, deal directly with dog exhibitors, breeders or judges. For information pertaining to breeders, clubs or shows, please contact the relevant State or Territory Body.

International
Fédération Cynologique Internationalé (FCI)
Place Albert 1er, 13, B-6530 Thuin, Belgium.
Tel: +32 71 59.12.38
Fax: +32 71 59.22.29
Web: www.fci.be

Training and behavior
UK
Association of Pet Dog Trainers
Telephone: 01285 810811
Web: www.apdt.co.uk

Association of Pet Behaviour Counsellors
Telephone: 01386 751151
Web: www.apbc.org.uk

USA
Association of Pet Dog Trainers
Tel: 1 800 738 3647
Web: www.apdt.com

American College of Veterinary Behaviorists
Web: www.dacvb.org

American Veterinary Society of Animal Behavior
Web: www.avsabonline.org

Australia
APDT Australia Inc
Web: www.apdt.com.au

Canine Behavior
For details of regional behvaiourists, contact the relevant State or Territory Controlling Body.

Activities

UK

Agility Club
Web: www.agilityclub.co.uk

British Flyball Association
Telephone: 01628 829623
Web: www.flyball.org.uk

USA

North American Dog Agility Council
Web: www.nadac.com

North American Flyball Association, Inc.
Tel/Fax: 800 318 6312
Web: www.flyball.org

Australia

Agility Dog Association of Australia
Tel: 0423 138 914
Web: www.adaa.com.au

NADAC Australia (North American Dog
Agility Council - Australian Division)
Web: www.nadacaustralia.com

Australian Flyball Association
Tel: 0407 337 939
Web: www.flyball.org.au

International

World Canine Freestyle Organisation
Tel: (718) 332-8336
Web: www.worldcaninefreestyle.org

Health

UK

British Small Animal Veterinary Association
Tel: 01452 726700
Web: www.bsava.com

Royal College of Veterinary Surgeons
Tel: 0207 222 2001
Web: www.rcvs.org.uk

Alternative Veterinary Medicine Centre
Tel: 01367 710324
Web: www.alternativevet.org

USA

American Veterinary Medical Association
Tel: 800 248 2862
Web: www.avma.org

American College of Veterinary Surgeons
Tel: 301 916 0200
Toll Free: 877 217 2287
Web: www.acvs.org

Canine Eye Registration Foundation
The Veterinary Medical DataBases
1717 Philo Rd, PO Box 3007,
Urbana, IL 61803-3007
Tel: 217-693-4800
Fax: 217-693-4801
Web: www.vmdb.org/cerf.html

Orthopaedic Foundation of Animals
2300 E Nifong Boulevard
Columbia, Missouri, 65201-3806
Tel: 573 442-0418
Fax: 573 875-5073
Web: www.offa.org

American Holistic Veterinary Medical
Association
Tel: 410 569 0795
Web: www.ahvma.org

Australia

Australian Small Animal Veterinary
Association
Tel: 02 9431 5090
Web: www.asava.com.au

Australian Veterinary Association
Tel: 02 9431 5000
Web: www.ava.com.au

Australian College Veterinary Scientists
Tel: 07 3423 2016
Web: www.acvsc.org.au

Australian Holistic Vets
Web: www.ahv.com.au

The Labrador Retriever